The Camping Cookbook

The Camping COOKbook

First published in 2009
Love Food ® is an imprint of Parragon Books Ltd

Parragon
Queen Street House
4 Queen Street
Bath BA1 1HE, UK

ISBN: 978-1-4075-6250-6

Printed in China

Project managed by Natalie Coates
Front cover and internal design by Lexi L'Esteve
Photography by Mike Cooper
Insert photography by Jim Johnston
Home economy by Lincoln Jefferson
Additional photography by Sian Irvine
Additional home economy by Katie Giovanni
Text and additional recipes by Rachel Carter

Special thanks to Ben, Benedict, Lucy and Polly.

Notes for the Reader
This book uses both metric and imperial measurements. Follow the same units of measurement throughout; do not mix metric and imperial. All spoon measurements are level: teaspoons are assumed to be 5 ml, and tablespoons are assumed to be 15 ml. Unless otherwise stated, milk is assumed to be full fat, eggs and individual vegetables are medium, and pepper is freshly ground black pepper.

The times given are an approximate guide only. Preparation times differ according to the techniques used by different people and the cooking times may also vary from those given due to the nature of campsite cooking. Optional ingredients, variations or serving suggestions have not been included in the calculations.

Recipes using raw or very lightly cooked eggs should be avoided by infants, the elderly, pregnant women, convalescents and anyone suffering from an illness. Pregnant and breastfeeding women are advised to avoid eating peanuts and peanut products. Sufferers from nut allergies should be aware that some of the ready-made ingredients used in the recipes in this book may contain nuts. Always check the packaging before use.

Contents

Foreword
by Stefan Gates

Something magical happens when you're camping: your appetite becomes immense and your enjoyment of food increases tenfold. It's partly because your senses are aroused by the sounds, smells and sights of the outdoors, but it's also the sheer liberation of escaping the kitchen and eating simple food that matches your resources. Above all, there's a caveman-esque exhilaration in feasting around a fire, even if it's just a little gas-powered one.

I've had some extraordinary camping meals whilst filming *Cooking in the Danger Zone* for the BBC: barbecued lamb's testicles in Afghanistan, burned rat in India and grilled palm weevils in Cameroon. The strangest meal was cooked under the bristling machine-guns of rebel soldiers whilst hiding from enemy patrols in the snake-infested jungles of Eastern Burma. I was exhausted and terrified when we stopped to camp but instead of hiding in the bush, the rebels took out their machetes and taught me to hack cups, spoons and saucepans out of bamboo, before sitting down to a supper of foraged jungle food. Nothing was going to stop them from enjoying their dinner.

You don't need lots of cash to eat like a king when camping. You just need the resolve to avoid stocking up on ready-meals and instead to arm yourself with a decently stocked storecupboard, a few great, fresh ingredients from local shops and a book like this one for the inspiration and expertise to throw together a brilliant meal. With love and enthusiasm (and a small fire), the caveman inside you awakens and every camping meal becomes a little feast.

Stefan Gates

Getting Started

Whether you're off to a music festival or just spending time with friends and family, camping captures the idealistic notion of enjoying nature and getting away from the busy pace of modern life. Troubles seem forgotten and worries disappear as you settle into a way of living that you can never quite create elsewhere. Living under canvas is great fun – you quickly realize that you can live without the television, the Internet, and all the mod cons that are part and parcel of daily life. Stripped back to the basics, everyday living is really quite simple.

When buying your camping equipment, you don't need every gadget going – start with the basics and wait and see whether you enjoy it first. Whatever your budget, you'll find something to suit you either in department stores and speciality outdoor shops or online.

The tent will naturally be your biggest purchase. If you are planning longer trips away, choose one large enough to be able to stand up in and eat in if the weather is bad. If your budget allows, buy bigger than you need – those extra bedrooms will prove invaluable to store things in!

Other key items will be the bedding (air bed, roll mat or both) plus sleeping bags, and your cooking equipment. Holdalls with plenty of compartments for clothes, toiletries, etc., are also essential. Finally, a good set of collapsible chairs and a table that won't fold up whilst you're eating your meal are worth investing in.

Eating outdoors is always a highlight of the summer months and food somehow tastes better after a day in the fresh air. A gazebo to erect next to your tent can be handy as an extra item of shelter (from rain or sun) to eat under. It also makes a good communal area in which to chat and drink in the evenings with your fellow campers.

There's a huge range of nifty cooking equipment available, from the humble individual gas burner to disposable barbecues (perfect for beach or cliff-top barbecues), to top of the range Australian-style gas-powered barbecues designed to be truly portable and capable of cooking a meal for the whole family in one go. These are especially good for making a hearty breakfast, as everything can be cooked on the hot plate so washing up is kept to a minimum. The main thing to remember is to choose your equipment based on the number of people you're cooking for – an individual gas burner will not be sufficient for a family feast!

Try planning a few meals before you go away, and make sure you discuss food ideas with everyone who's involved in the camping trip (saves a lot of arguing later on!). Then all the meals can be sorted in advance so all that's required are a few clever storecupboard ingredients and maybe some fresh and frozen items taken from home, combined with some freshly bought produce each day. All that's left is to cook, eat and enjoy!

*see next page

Equipment List

1 = grater

2 = washing-up liquid

3 = tea towel

4 = kitchen roll

5 = dishcloth

6 = salt and pepper

7 = cutlery

8 = wooden spoons

9 = bag of charcoal

10 = aluminium foil

11 = clingfilm

12 = greaseproof paper

13 = sharp knife

14 = corkscrew

15 = chopping board

16 = shallow pan

17 = folding camping toaster

18 = small non-stick frying pan

19 = mugs/plastic glasses

20 = vegetable chopping board

21 = barbecue tongs

22 = heatproof bowls

23 = pocket knife

24 = potato masher

25 = skewers

26 = eggcups

27 = meat choppping board

28 = chopping knife

29 = serving bowls

30 = plates

31 = mess tins

32 = medium saucepan

33 = small saucepan

34 = large non-stick frying pan

35 = cool box

Hints & Tips For Pitching Your Tent

Before you get to your campsite, it's always worth having a test run with your tent in the garden. If it proves tricky, then take some digital photos of the tent as it goes up which you can then print off and keep with the instructions. Colour coding poles might also be useful.

When you get to your campsite, choosing your pitch is vital. Try and avoid anywhere that looks wet and boggy. It's also important to look for shade from the wind and/or sun and try to avoid pitching up right beside the toilet or washing blocks. Do a complete 'poo patrol' before settling on a spot – whether it's the cow or dog variety, you don't want it walked through your tent!

Check that you have enough room to park alongside your tent and make sure you like the look of your neighbours – if they look like party types, chances are they'll keep you up at night. Also check that the water supply and toilet blocks are not too far away.

A level pitch is preferable, and check that there are no sharp stones or tree roots in the vicinity that might poke through your ground sheet and tear a hole. An extra groundsheet can be useful to put down, as it will protect the sewn-in one from damage.

Buy some spare tent pegs to take with you as campsites always overcharge in their shops. Also an extra rubber mallet can be handy, especially if your tent is large, as this will help to speed up the pitching process.

Make sure that the children are well occupied while you're putting up your tent – it can be quite stressful, especially if the weather is bad. This might be the time to bring out a new DVD to watch on the portable player or a simple game to play in the car.

Campsite Cooking

cooking with gas

The simplest way of cooking is on a basic gas stove. These start with a basic one-burner version, which uses a small gas canister and is ideal for boiling a kettle or perhaps heating a tin of beans in a saucepan.

For a little more versatility, try a small camp cooker. These are collapsible, often supplied in a handy carrying bag and with either two or three burners and usually a small grill and wind protection around the sides. This size is suitable for a wide variety of meals and most of the recipes in this book.

If you're getting serious about camping and you're away for more than a weekend then you may need a 'camp kitchen'. This is a purpose-built stand on which your gas stove can be stored with plenty of shelves underneath for all your food and equipment.

cooking on the barbecue

At a very basic level, disposable barbecues are so inexpensive that they are perfect for a night or two away if you don't want the hassle of getting an authentic barbecue started. These are ideal for cooking a small breakfast or evening meal. You can now buy a custom-made stand to hold these mini barbecues above the ground, which prevents the grass from scorching. Inspired by Argentinian cowboys, the 'Asado' stand is a cool and stylish addition to your camping equipment.

If you want to use charcoal to start your own barbecue, then there are plenty of reasonably priced barbecues which can be quickly assembled, including the bucket-style barbecue. These are cheap

to buy, with folding legs for easy storage and are ideal for cooking a range of foods such as sausages, steaks or fish, whether it's on the campsite or the beach. They heat up quickly and retain heat, making them small but brilliantly efficient.

If you want to spend a little more, gas-powered barbecues are extremely efficient as well as being easy to use and clean. They have the added benefit of providing instant heat if you need to eat in a hurry. At the top end of the market are very sophisticated models with interchangeable cooking surfaces, a stove and a reversible non-stick grill among other features. These models are hugely versatile and portable and are ideal when cooking for larger numbers of people. Whatever your needs and choice, try and buy from a reputable dealer where you should be guaranteed a quality appliance that will last the course.

cooking over the campfire

Cooking over the campfire is perhaps the most idealistic vision of cooking outdoors. In reality, it is a little more tricky to conquer, as some campsites don't allow campfires and you can't rely on adjusting the heat source as you would with a gas stove. It is, however, hard to beat the taste of food cooked over a campfire, especially if you add some flavoured woodchips to give your food a smoky or spicy taste (instructions on how to use the woodchips can be found on the back of their packet). And marshmallows popped on the end of a skewer and toasted around the campfire as night falls will always delight, no matter what your age.

Campfire cooking requires a clean-burning, hot fire. This is only achieved with dry, seasoned wood – if the wood is damp, your fire will be smoky and will burn poorly. The same thing goes for any sign of a medium-strong wind – unless you are well sheltered, this is one battle you will not win. If conditions are favourable, a camping grill rack or griddle placed over the fire will cook your food to perfection. This method of cooking requires constant attention to ensure that the food doesn't catch fire, and be sure to wait until the fire is beginning to die off before you start cooking, as otherwise the heat will be too strong.

'Don't Forget' Check List

Toilet rolls

Matches

Torch

Bin bags

Anti-bacterial wet wipes

Liquid soap (the one which works without water is best)

Clothes pegs and washing line

Pocket mirror

Spare batteries for torch

First aid kit

Radio (wind-up is best)

Water carrier

Wellingtons

Sun cream

Storecupboard Essentials

Prepare these two little gems before you set off and you'll have lots of lunch and dinner ideas for your trip – minimum fuss required.

Heat the tomato sauce and add as a topping to jacket potatoes with plenty of grated cheese

Slice open a bagel, toast o the campfire, spread with the tomato sauce and ad thick wedges of cheese f a heart-warming lunch

fresh tomato sauce

Stir through pasta, and add some mince and chopped onions for a speedy Spaghetti Bolognese

Fry some sliced courgettes, peppers and red onion and sti through the warmed sauce fo a quick ratatouille

makes about 600 ml/1 pint
1 tbsp olive oil
1 small onion, chopped
2–3 garlic cloves, crushed (optional)
1 small celery stick, finely chopped
1 bay leaf
450 g/1 lb ripe tomatoes, peeled and chopped
1 tbsp tomato purée, blended with 150 ml/5 fl oz water
few sprigs fresh oregano
pepper

Heat the oil in a heavy-based saucepan, add the onion, garlic, if using, celery and bay leaf, and gently sauté, stirring frequently, for 5 minutes.

Stir in the tomatoes with the blended tomato purée. Add pepper to taste and the oregano. Bring to the boil, then reduce the heat, cover and simmer, stirring occasionally, for 20–25 minutes until the tomatoes have completely collapsed. If liked, simmer for a further 20 minutes to give a thicker sauce.

Discard the bay leaf and the oregano. Transfer to a food processor and process to a chunky purée. If a smooth sauce is preferred, pass through a fine non-metallic sieve. Taste and adjust the seasoning if necessary. Reheat and use as required.

Stir through pasta, add some Parmesan shavings and enjoy

Add to mash for a s-mashing side

basil pesto

Serve with a tin of tuna and add as a topping to jacket potatoes

Stir through freshly-boiled new potatoes and top with trusty Parmesan

Slice open a ciabatta roll, toast on the campfire, spread with pesto and add some cream cheese and sun-dried tomatoes for a yummy lunch

makes about 225 g/8 oz
55 g/2 oz fresh basil leaves
1 garlic clove
25 g/1 oz toasted pine kernels
125–150 ml/4–5 fl oz extra virgin olive oil
25 g/1 oz freshly grated Parmesan cheese
1–2 tsp freshly squeezed lemon juice (optional)
salt and pepper

Tear the basil leaves and put in a large mortar with the garlic, pine kernels and 1 tablespoon of the oil. Pound with a pestle to form a paste.

Gradually work in the remaining oil to form a thick sauce. Add salt and pepper to taste and stir in the Parmesan cheese. If liked, slacken slightly with the lemon juice.

The Big Breakfast

Bacon Butties

Serves 1

4 smoked bacon rashers

1 tbsp olive oil

15 g/½ oz butter, softened

2 slices thick white or brown
bread

1 tomato, sliced (optional)

sauce of choice (brown sauce,
tomato sauce or mustard)

pepper

Cut the rashers in half. Add the oil to a non-stick frying pan and cook the bacon over a campfire, stove or barbecue until cooked to your liking. Meanwhile, butter the bread. Place 2 pieces of bacon on one slice of bread and season with a grinding of pepper. Add the tomato, if using, and the sauce. Top with the remaining bacon and the other slice of bread and eat immediately. A serious contender for the best breakfast ever.

Breakfast Bagels

Serves 4

4 large open-cup mushrooms
½ tbsp olive oil
4 eggs
4 bagels, halved and toasted
salt and pepper

Remove the entire stalk from the mushrooms.
Cut out a small hollow from below each stalk using the tip of a
small sharp knife to make room for the egg to be added.

Place the oil in a non-stick frying pan and warm over a campfire,
stove or barbecue. Add the mushrooms 2 at a time with the
hollowed side facing up. Cook gently for 4–5 minutes turning once
until they start to soften.

Crack an egg into the hollow of each mushroom, season and cook
for a further 6–8 minutes or until the eggs are cooked to your
liking. Repeat with the remaining mushrooms.

Serve the egg-filled mushrooms on the toasted bagels.

Toasted Muffins with Honey-glazed Bacon & Eggs

Serves 2

1 tbsp olive oil

6 rindless unsmoked bacon rashers

1 tbsp clear honey

85 g/3 oz canned sweetcorn kernels, drained

2 small tomatoes, diced

1 tbsp chopped fresh parsley

4 eggs

2 muffins, split, toasted and buttered

salt and pepper

Place the oil in a non-stick frying pan and warm over a campfire, stove or barbecue. Gently cook the bacon until lightly browned. Turn and cook on the other side.

Slightly warm the honey and brush each rasher lightly with it. Cook the bacon for a further 1 minute or so until it takes on a slight glaze. Remove from the pan and wrap the bacon in aluminium foil to keep warm.

Mix together the sweetcorn, diced tomatoes and chopped parsley and season to taste with salt and pepper. Fry, poach or scramble the eggs, as you prefer.

Serve the honey-glazed bacon and eggs on the toasted muffins, topped with a spoonful of the sweetcorn and tomato mixture.

Why Skipping Breakfast Is Bad For You

Tempting though it may be to bounce out of your air bed in the morning and get straight into the next activity, it is well documented that missing breakfast is a big mistake. Here are some reasons why you shouldn't skip the first meal of the day.

Sharing a cooked breakfast or just a bacon sandwich with your friends and family is a serious bonding experience (and the smell of bacon will drive your neighbours mad!).

If you're suffering from a camping hangover, then a good well-balanced breakfast will soon have you on the mend.

It's a great opportunity to eat well and discuss the plans for the day ahead.

Set your children a good example. Eating breakfast is known to help concentration levels, and when they're back at school it's a good routine to keep to.

Eating first thing will put you in a better mood for the day ahead – remember, you're on holiday; you will have a good time!

Breakfast in the outdoors on a campsite is an education in itself. We guarantee that the sights and sounds of other campers waking up and going about their everyday chores will be enough to make you appreciate the simple things in life.

It's potentially the best meal of the day. Bacon, eggs – need we say more?!

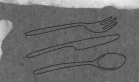

Apple & Spice Porridge

Serves 4

600 ml/1 pint milk or water

1 tsp salt

115 g/4 oz medium rolled
porridge oats

2 large apples

½ tsp ground mixed spice

honey (optional), to serve

Put the milk in a saucepan and bring to the boil over a campfire, stove or barbecue. Add the salt and sprinkle in the oats, stirring constantly.

Place over a low heat and leave the oats to simmer for 10 minutes, stirring occasionally.

Meanwhile, halve, core and grate the apples. When the porridge is creamy and most of the liquid has evaporated, stir in the grated apple and mixed spice. Spoon into bowls and drizzle with the honey, if using. Serve on a chilly morning for instant warmth.

Greek Yogurt with Honey, Nuts & Blueberries

Serves 4

3 tbsp clear honey

100 g/3½ oz mixed unsalted nuts

8 tbsp Greek yogurt

200 g/7 oz fresh blueberries

Gently heat the honey in a small saucepan over a campfire, stove or barbecue, add the nuts and stir until they are well coated. Remove from the heat and leave to cool slightly.

Divide the yogurt between 4 bowls, then spoon over the nut mixture and blueberries.

Spicy Fried Eggs

Serves 2

2 tbsp olive oil

1 large onion, finely chopped

2 green or red peppers, deseeded
and roughly chopped

1 garlic clove, finely chopped

½ tsp dried chilli flakes

4 plum tomatoes, peeled and
roughly chopped

2 eggs

salt and pepper

Heat the oil in a large non-stick frying pan over a campfire, stove or barbecue. Add the onion and cook until golden. Add the peppers, garlic and chilli flakes and cook until the peppers are soft.

Stir in the tomatoes and season to taste with salt and pepper. Place over a low heat and simmer for 10 minutes.

Using the back of a spoon, make 2 depressions in the mixture in the frying pan. Break the eggs into the depressions, season if liked and cover and cook for 3-4 minutes until the eggs are set. Serve.

Scrambled Eggs with Smoked Salmon

Serves 4

8 eggs

90 ml/3 fl oz single cream

2 tbsp chopped fresh dill,
plus extra for garnishing

100 g/3½ oz smoked salmon,
cut into small pieces

25 g/1 oz butter

8 slices rustic bread, toasted

salt and pepper

Break the eggs into a large bowl and whisk together with the cream and dill. Season to taste with salt and pepper. Add the smoked salmon and mix to combine.

Melt the butter in a large non-stick frying pan over a campfire, stove or barbecue and pour in the egg and smoked salmon mixture. Gently scrape the egg away from the sides of the pan as it begins to set and swirl the pan slightly to allow the uncooked egg to fill the surface. When the eggs are almost cooked but still creamy, remove from the heat and spoon onto the prepared toast. Serve immediately with the dill.

Chipotle Beans & Sausages

Serves 4

1 tbsp vegetable oil

8 chipolata pork sausages

2 x 415 g/14½ oz cans baked beans

½ tsp chipotle paste (or use a pinch of smoked paprika & pinch of dried chilli flakes)

100 g/3½ oz mature Cheddar cheese, grated

salt and pepper

Heat the oil in a non-stick frying pan over a campfire, stove or barbecue and fry the sausages for 15–20 minutes until golden brown and thoroughly cooked. Remove from the pan and cut into chunky pieces.

Add the baked beans and the chipotle paste to the pan, stir and heat through for 4–5 minutes until piping hot. Return the sausages to the pan and cook for another few minutes. Season to taste.

Serve the beans and sausages with the grated cheese sprinkled over the top.

Mini Damper Bread Rolls

Makes about 8

275 g/9¾ oz self-raising flour

½ tsp salt

175 ml/6 fl oz milk

2 tbsp clear honey

olive oil, to grease

butter and jam, to serve

Put the flour into a bowl, add the salt and make a well in the centre.

Combine the milk and honey then add to the flour and, using a knife, mix well into a dough. Use your hands to shape the dough into 8 small patties. Lightly oil a non-stick frying pan and cook the patties over a campfire, stove or around the edge of the barbecue for about 10 minutes until a crust has formed and the centre is just cooked (test by tapping the base with your fingers. If it sounds hollow, then it is cooked). Turn regularly to prevent burning.

Serve halved with plenty of butter and jam.

Apple Pancakes with Maple Syrup

Makes 18

200 g/7 oz self-raising flour
100 g/3½ oz caster sugar
1 tsp ground cinnamon
1 egg
200 ml/7 fl oz milk
2 apples, peeled and grated
1 tsp butter
3 tbsp maple syrup

Mix together the flour, sugar and cinnamon in a bowl and make a well in the centre. Beat together the egg and the milk and pour into the well. Using a wooden spoon, gently incorporate the dry ingredients into the liquid until well combined, then stir in the grated apple.

Gently heat the butter in a large non-stick frying pan over a campfire, stove or barbecue until melted and bubbling. Add tablespoons of the pancake mixture to form small circles. Cook each pancake for about 1 minute, until it starts to bubble lightly on the top and looks set, then flip it over and cook the other side for 30 seconds, or until cooked through. The pancakes should be golden brown. Remove from the pan and wrap the pancakes in aluminium foil to keep warm. Repeat the process until all of the pancake batter has been used up (it is not necessary to add extra butter). Serve with the maple syrup drizzled over and around the pancakes. Enjoy!

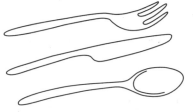

French Toast with Maple Syrup

Serves 4–6

6 eggs

175 ml/6 fl oz milk

¼ tsp ground cinnamon

12 slices day-old plain white bread

about 2 tbsp butter or margarine, plus extra to serve

½ –1 tbsp sunflower or corn oil

salt

maple syrup, to serve

Break the eggs into a large, shallow bowl and beat together with the milk, cinnamon and salt to taste. Add the bread slices and press them down so that they are covered on both sides with the egg mixture. Leave the bread to stand for 1–2 minutes to soak up the egg mixture, turning the slices over once.

Melt the butter with half a tablespoon of oil in a large non-stick frying pan over a campfire, stove or barbecue. Add to the pan as many bread slices as will fit in a single layer and cook for 2–3 minutes until golden brown.

Turn the bread slices over and cook until golden brown on the other side. Wrap the cooked bread in aluminium foil to keep warm and repeat with the remaining bread. Add any extra oil if necessary.

Serve the toast with the maple syrup.

Lunchtime

Bread & Tomato Soup

Serves 6

450 g/1 lb two-day-old
crusty bread
1 kg/2 lb 4 oz plum tomatoes
4 tbsp olive oil
4 garlic cloves, crushed
500 ml/18 fl oz boiling water
1 bunch fresh basil
salt and pepper
6 tbsp extra virgin olive oil,
to serve

Cut the bread into slices and then cubes (you can remove some of the crusts if you wish) and leave to dry out for 30 minutes. Meanwhile, peel the tomatoes and cut into chunks.

Gently heat the olive oil in a large saucepan over a campfire, stove or barbecue, add the garlic and stir for 1 minute. Add the tomatoes and gently simmer for 20–30 minutes until the mixture has thickened.

Add the bread and stir until it has absorbed the liquid. Stir in the boiling water until you have a thick soupy mixture. Season well with salt and pepper.

Remove the basil leaves from their stems and tear any large leaves into pieces. Stir the basil into the soup.

Serve warm with a tablespoonful of extra virgin olive oil sprinkled over each bowl.

Chicken Noodle Soup

Serves 4–6

2 skinless chicken breasts

1.2 litres/2 pints water or
chicken stock

3 carrots, peeled and sliced into
5-mm/¼-inch slices

85 g/3 oz vermicelli (or other
small noodles)

salt and pepper

Place the chicken breasts in a large saucepan, add the water and bring to a simmer over a campfire, stove or barbecue. Cook for 25–30 minutes. Skim any scum from the surface if necessary. Remove the chicken from the stock and wrap the chicken in aluminium foil to keep warm.

Continue to simmer the stock, add the carrots and vermicelli and cook for 4–5 minutes.

Thinly slice the chicken breasts and place in mugs or bowls.

Season the soup to taste with salt and pepper and pour over the chicken. Serve. A perfect meal in a mug!

Cheesy Sweetcorn Fritters

Makes 8–10 small fritters

1 egg

200 ml/7 fl oz milk

100 g/3½ oz plain flour

½ tsp baking powder

85 g/3 oz canned sweetcorn kernels, drained

4 tbsp grated Cheddar cheese

1 tsp snipped fresh chives

2 tsp sunflower oil

Put the egg and milk into a small bowl and beat with a fork. Add the flour and baking powder and beat until smooth. Stir in the sweetcorn, cheese and chives. Heat the sunflower oil in a non-stick frying pan over a campfire, stove or barbecue. Drop in either teaspoonfuls or tablespoonfuls of the batter. Cook for 1–2 minutes on each side until the fritters are puffed up and golden.

Drain on kitchen paper and serve.

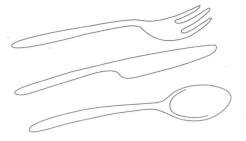

Spinach & Mozzarella Omelette

Serves 4

1 tbsp oil
1 tbsp butter
4 eggs, beaten lightly
40 g/1½ oz mozzarella cheese, thinly sliced and cut into bite-sized pieces
small handful baby spinach, stalks removed
salt and pepper

Heat the oil in a large non-stick saucepan over a campfire, stove or barbecue. Add the butter and when it sizzles, pour in the eggs. Season with salt and pepper, then gently stir with the back of a fork until large flakes form. Leave to cook for a few seconds then tilt the pan and lift the edges of the mixture with a knife, so that uncooked egg flows underneath to cook evenly.

Scatter the cheese and spinach over the top, and leave to cook for a few seconds. Once the surface starts to solidify, carefully fold the omelette in half. Cook for a few seconds, pressing the surface with the back of a knife. Turn the omelette over and cook for another few seconds, until the cheese is soft and the spinach wilted.

Slip the omelette onto a plate and slice into segments. Serve warm or cold.

Tomato Bruschetta

Serves 4

8 slices rustic bread, toasted

4 garlic cloves, halved

8 plum tomatoes, peeled and
diced

extra virgin olive oil, for
drizzling

salt and pepper

fresh basil leaves,to garnish

Rub each piece of toast with half a garlic clove.

Divide the diced tomatoes between the toasts. Season to taste
with salt and pepper and drizzle with olive oil. Serve immediately,
garnished with basil leaves.

Cheesy Chicken & Chutney Toasties

Serves 4

8 thin slices wholemeal or granary bread

2 tsp soft butter

200 g/7 oz cooked sliced chicken

100 g/3½ oz mature Cheddar cheese

8 tbsp fruity chutney, such as apple and fig

Heat a non-stick frying pan over a campfire, stove or barbecue. Spread one side of each slice of the bread with a little butter.

To make each sandwich, place one slice of bread buttered side down in the hot frying pan and add the chicken and cheese. Spread 2 tbsp of the chutney over the unbuttered side of the other slice of the bread, place on top of the sandwich and press down firmly.

Cook over a moderate heat for 2–3 minutes on each side so that the bread is lightly toasted and the cheese melted.

Repeat with the remaining bread and serve. Vary the fillings according to individual tastes.

Beef & Stilton wraps

Serves 4

250 g/9 oz sirloin steak
1 tbsp olive oil
1 tbsp mayonnaise
125 g/4½ oz Stilton cheese,
crumbled
4 x 25-cm/10-inch wraps
salt and pepper

Season the steak with salt and pepper.

Heat a non-stick frying pan until almost smoking over a campfire, stove or barbecue. Add the oil, and then seal the steak, cooking on both sides for 30 seconds. Remove from the pan and set aside for a few minutes. Once the steak has rested, cut into thin strips with a sharp knife.

Mix together the mayonnaise and Stilton cheese.

If the pan has cooled, reheat again until almost smoking, then cook the wraps one at a time on both sides for 10 seconds. This will add some colour and also soften the wraps.

Divide the steak between the wraps, placing it along the middle of each wrap. Top with the Stilton and mayonnaise. Roll up, cut in half and serve.

Campfire Quesadillas

Serves 1

2 flour tortillas

1–2 tbsp tomato salsa

25 g/1 oz freshly grated Manchego or other hard cheese

4 slices chopped chorizo

Heat a non-stick frying pan over a campfire, stove or barbecue until moderately hot.

Spread 1 of the tortillas with the salsa and place in the pan. Top with the cheese and chorizo and then top with the other tortilla. Allow to cook for 1–2 minutes until starting to turn golden on the base.

Flip the quesadilla over using a knife and cook for a further 1–2 minutes to allow the cheese to melt and the base of the tortilla to brown lightly.

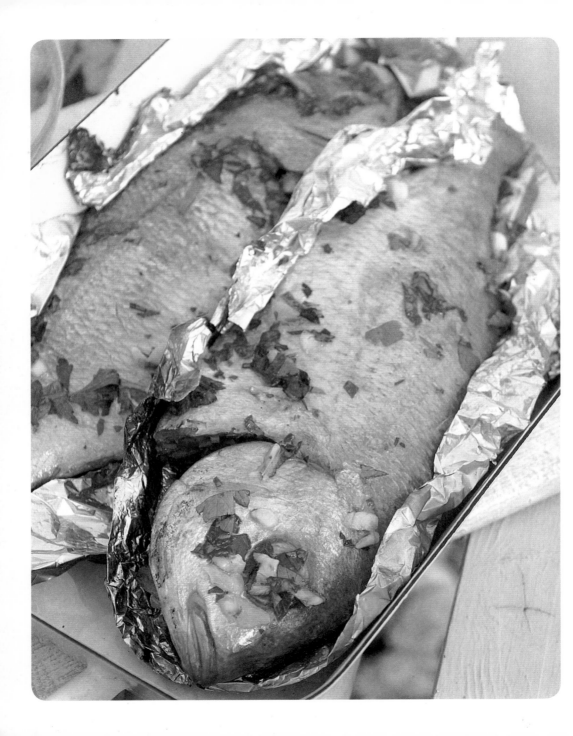

Baked Snapper

Serves 4

2 bunches fresh basil
85 g/3 oz butter, softened
4 garlic cloves, crushed
4 red snapper or red mullet,
about 350 g/12 oz each, scaled,
trimmed and cleaned
salt and pepper

Cut out 4 squares of double-thickness aluminium foil, each large enough to hold a whole fish.

Reserve 4 basil sprigs for the garnish and chop the remaining basil. Cream the butter in a bowl with a wooden spoon, then beat in the chopped basil and the garlic.

Season the fish inside and out with salt and pepper. Put 1 fish on a piece of foil. Spoon one quarter of the basil and garlic butter into the cavity and wrap the foil around the fish to enclose it completely. Repeat with the remaining fish.

Put the fish parcels on a campfire or over the barbecue for 25–30 minutes, or until the fish flakes easily when tested with the point of a knife. Transfer the fish parcels to plates and unwrap. Carefully slide out the fish and the cooking juices onto the plates and serve immediately.

Normandy Cream Mussels

Serves 4

2 kg/4 lb 8 oz live mussels

300 ml/10 fl oz dry cider

6 shallots, finely chopped

6 tbsp double cream

pepper

Scrub the mussels under cold running water, scraping off any barnacles with a knife, and pull off the beards. Discard any mussels with broken shells or open ones that do not shut immediately when sharply tapped with the handle of a knife.

Pour the cider into a flameproof casserole dish, add the shallots and season with pepper. Bring to the boil over a campfire, stove or barbecue and cook for 2 minutes.

Add the mussels, cover with a tight-fitting lid and cook over a high heat, shaking the casserole dish occasionally, for about 5 minutes until the shells have opened. Remove the mussels with a slotted spoon, discarding any that remain closed, and keep warm.

Strain the cooking liquid into a saucepan. Bring to the boil and cook for 8–10 minutes until reduced by about half. Stir in the cream and add the mussels. Cook for 1 minute to reheat the shellfish, then serve.

Chicken Satay Skewers

Serves 4

4 tbsp smooth peanut butter

100 ml/3½ fl oz soy sauce

4 skinless, boneless chicken
breasts, cut into thin strips

If using wooden kebab skewers, soak 1 per person in cold water for
30 minutes first to prevent burning.

Mix together the peanut butter and soy sauce in a bowl
until smooth. Stir in the chicken strips, tossing well to coat in
the mixture.

Thread the chicken strips onto the pre-soaked wooden skewers
and cook over a campfire or barbecue until cooked through. Serve.

Bubble & Squeak

Serves 4

450 g/1 lb floury potatoes, diced

225 g/8 oz Savoy cabbage, shredded

5 tbsp vegetable oil

2 leeks, chopped

1 garlic clove, crushed

225 g/8 oz smoked tofu, drained and diced

salt and pepper

shredded cooked leek, to garnish

Cook the potatoes in a saucepan of lightly salted, boiling water over a campfire, stove or barbecue, for 10 minutes. Drain and mash the potatoes.

Meanwhile, in a separate saucepan, blanch the cabbage in boiling water for 5 minutes. Drain well and add to the potato.

Heat the oil in a large non-stick frying pan. Add the leeks and garlic and fry over a low heat for 2–3 minutes. Stir into the potato and cabbage mixture.

Add the smoked tofu and season well with salt and pepper. Cook over a high heat for 10 minutes.

Carefully turn the whole mixture over and continue to cook for 5–7 minutes more, until it is crispy underneath.

Serve immediately, garnished with shredded leek.

Ratatouille with Poached Eggs

Serves 4

2 tbsp olive oil

1 large onion, sliced

2 peppers, any colour, deseeded and thinly sliced

2 courgettes, sliced into thin rounds

1 small aubergine, halved lengthways and thinly sliced

2 garlic cloves, chopped

300 ml/10 fl oz passata with herbs, plus extra if needed

2 tsp smoked paprika

8 small eggs

salt and pepper

Gently heat the oil in a large, lidded, non-stick frying pan over a campfire, stove or barbecue. Add the onion and peppers and cook, stirring frequently, for 4–5 minutes, until beginning to soften.

Add the courgettes, aubergine and garlic and cook, stirring, for 2 minutes. Add the passata, most of the paprika and a little salt and pepper to taste. Stir and bring to a simmer. Place over a low heat, cover and leave to simmer gently for 45 minutes, adding a little extra passata or water if the mixture begins to look dry.

Make 8 wells in the ratatouille and break an egg into each. Re-cover and cook for a further 10 minutes, or until the egg whites are cooked but the yolks are still runny.

Serve immediately, garnished with paprika.

Pan Potato Cake

Serves 4

675 g/1½ lb waxy potatoes, unpeeled and sliced

1 carrot, diced

225 g/8 oz small broccoli florets

5 tbsp butter

2 tbsp vegetable oil

1 red onion, quartered

2 garlic cloves, crushed

175 g/6 oz firm tofu, drained and diced

2 tbsp chopped fresh sage

75 g/2¾ oz mature cheese, grated

Cook the sliced potatoes in a large saucepan of boiling water over a campfire, stove or barbecue for 10 minutes. Drain thoroughly.

Meanwhile, cook the carrot and broccoli florets in a separate pan of boiling water for 5 minutes. Drain.

Heat the butter and oil in a large non-stick frying pan. Add the onion and garlic and gently fry for 2–3 minutes. Add half of the potato slices to the frying pan, covering the base of the pan.

Cover the potato slices with the carrot, broccoli and tofu. Sprinkle with the sage and cover with the remaining potato slices. Sprinkle the grated cheese over the top.

Cook over a high heat for 8–10 minutes. Cover the pan with a piece of aluminium foil for 5–6 minutes until the cheese melts and browns. Serve and enjoy.

Meat Feast Muffin Pizzas

Serves 4

4 tbsp pizza base sauce (or tomato purée)

4 wholemeal or white muffins, halved

2 tbsp olives, stoned and chopped

3 button mushrooms, finely sliced

100 g/3½ oz pepperoni sausage, thinly sliced

125 g/4½ oz mozzarella cheese, thinly sliced

Spread the pizza base sauce over the cut sides of the halved muffins.

Sprinkle over the olives, mushrooms and pepperoni.

Lay the mozzarella over the toppings and place the muffins (about 4 halves at a time) in a large non-stick frying pan. Tightly cover with foil and place over a campfire or barbecue for 8–10 minutes, checking regularly to ensure that the base is not burning and the cheese is melting.

Seriously Filling Dinners

Quick Chicken Laksa

Serves 4

850 ml/1½ pints canned coconut milk

200 ml/7 fl oz chicken stock

2–3 tbsp laksa paste

3 skinless, boneless chicken breasts, about 175 g/6 oz each, sliced into strips

250 g/9 oz cherry tomatoes, halved

250 g/9 oz sugar snap peas, halved diagonally

200 g/7 oz dried rice noodles

1 bunch fresh coriander, roughly chopped

Pour the coconut milk and stock into a saucepan and stir in the laksa paste. Add the chicken strips and gently simmer for 10–15 minutes over a campfire, stove or barbecue until the chicken is cooked through.

Stir in the tomatoes, sugar snap peas and noodles. Simmer for a further 2–3 minutes. Stir in the coriander and serve immediately. Speedy to cook and delicious to eat!

Irish Stew

Serves 4–6

1.3 kg/3 lb potatoes, peeled

1 kg/2 lb 4 oz best end of neck or other stewing lamb, trimmed of fat

500 g/1 lb 2 oz onions, thinly sliced

850 ml/1½ pints water

2 tbsp chopped fresh parsley

salt and pepper

Thinly slice half the potatoes. Make alternating layers of lamb, onions and sliced potatoes in a large, lidded, non-stick saucepan, seasoning each layer with salt and pepper. Pour in the water so that the layers are just covered.

Bring to the boil over a campfire, stove or barbecue. Place over a low heat, cover and gently simmer for 1³/4 hours. Cut the remaining potatoes into quarters and place on top of the stew to steam. Re-cover the pan and simmer for a further 45 minutes, or until the potato quarters are tender.

Arrange the steamed potatoes around the outside of a serving dish. Place the meat, onions and sliced potatoes in the centre. Taste the cooking liquid and adjust the seasoning, if necessary, then spoon it over the meat. Sprinkle with the parsley and serve immediately.

Chicken & Apricot Casserole

Serves 4

40 g/1½ oz plain flour

4 chicken portions

4 tbsp olive oil

350 g/12 oz dried apricots, soaked overnight in 600 ml/ 1 pint water

salt and pepper

Spread out the flour on a plate and season with salt and pepper. Roll the chicken portions in the flour to coat, shaking off any excess. Reserve the remaining seasoned flour.

Gently heat the oil in a flameproof casserole dish over a campfire, stove or barbecue. Add the chicken and cook, turning occasionally, for 8–10 minutes until golden brown. Remove with a slotted spoon and set aside.

Drain the apricots, reserving the soaking liquid. Add the reserved flour to the casserole dish and cook over a low heat, stirring constantly, for 2 minutes. Gradually stir in the reserved soaking liquid and bring to the boil, whilst stirring constantly.

Add the apricots and return the chicken to the casserole dish. Cover and gently simmer for 45 minutes, or until the chicken is tender and cooked through. Test by piercing the thickest part with the point of a knife. If the juices run clear, the chicken is ready. Serve immediately.

Creamy Ricotta, Mint & Garlic Pasta

Serves 4

300 g/10½ oz pasta shapes

140 g/5 oz ricotta cheese

1–2 roasted garlic cloves from a
jar, finely chopped

150 ml/5 fl oz double cream

1 tbsp chopped fresh mint

salt and pepper

Cook the pasta in a large saucepan of boiling salted water over a
campfire, stove or barbecue, until tender but still firm to the bite.

Beat together the ricotta, garlic, cream and chopped mint in a bowl
until smooth.

Drain the cooked pasta then tip back into the pan. Pour in the
cheese mixture and toss together.

Season with pepper and serve immediately.

Bad weather Blues
(And How To Beat Them)

People can be pretty resourceful when it comes to dealing with the weather and its unpredictability. But when you're camping and the weather is bad, sometimes a little bit of forward planning can make all the difference. Here are a few ideas on how to overcome those bad weather blues.

Before you set off, do some research on the Internet about places of interest nearby or days out. Print off some info and bring it with you on your camping trip.

Head to the nearest library. Here you can find out loads of local info, chat to the staff and use the Internet if you need to.

Pack a flask of hot chocolate and a kite on a blustery day; great fun.

Write a holiday diary. Popular with all ages, a simple journal with a few paragraphs about your activities each day and some postcards and leaflets stuck in will be lovely to look back on in years to come.

Play a few games in the tent if the weather is really bad. Charades and board games are always a hit. Or try making shadow puppets with a torch on the inside of the tent at night.

Penne Pasta with Sausage

Serves 4–6

2 tbsp olive oil
1 red onion, roughly chopped
2 garlic cloves, roughly chopped
6 Italian sausages, skinned and the meat crumbled
½ tsp dried chilli flakes
2 tbsp chopped fresh oregano
400 g/14 oz canned chopped tomatoes
350 g/12 oz dried penne
salt and pepper

Gently heat the oil in a large saucepan over a campfire, stove or barbecue. Add the onion and cook, stirring frequently, for 6–8 minutes until starting to brown. Add the garlic and the crumbled sausages and cook for 8–10 minutes, breaking up the sausages with a wooden spoon.

Add the chilli flakes and oregano and stir well. Pour in the tomatoes and bring to the boil. Place over a low heat and simmer for 4–5 minutes until reduced and thickened. Season to taste with salt and pepper.

Meanwhile, bring a large saucepan of salted water to the boil. Add the penne and stir well, return to the boil and cook for 10–12 minutes until tender but still firm to the bite. Drain well and return to the saucepan.

Pour the sauce into the pasta and stir well. Serve.

Chunky Potato & Spinach Curry

Serves 4

4 tomatoes

2 tbsp vegetable oil

2 onions, cut into thick wedges

2.5-cm/1-inch piece fresh ginger, peeled and finely chopped

1 garlic clove, chopped

2 tbsp ground coriander

450 g/1 lb potatoes, cut into chunks

600 ml/1 pint vegetable stock

1 tbsp Thai red curry paste

225 g/8 oz spinach leaves

salt and pepper

Put the tomatoes in a heatproof bowl and cover with boiling water. Leave for 2–3 minutes, then plunge into cold water and peel off the skins. Cut each tomato into quarters and remove and discard the seeds and central core. Set aside.

Gently heat the oil in a large non-stick frying pan over a campfire, stove or barbecue. Add the onions, ginger and garlic and fry for 2–3 minutes until starting to soften. Add the coriander and potatoes, place over a high heat and fry for 2–3 minutes. Add the stock and curry paste, season and bring to the boil, stirring occasionally. Place over a low heat and gently simmer for 10–15 minutes until the potatoes are tender.

Add the spinach and the tomato quarters and cook, stirring, for 1 minute, or until the spinach has wilted. Serve immediately.

Mushroom Stroganoff

Serves 4

25 g/1 oz butter

1 onion, finely chopped

450 g/1 lb closed-cup mushrooms, quartered

1 tsp tomato purée

1 tsp coarse-grain mustard

150 ml/5 fl oz crème fraîche

1 tsp paprika, plus extra to garnish

salt and pepper

Heat the butter in a large non-stick frying pan over a campfire, stove or barbecue. Add the onion and gently cook for 5–10 minutes, until soft.

Add the mushrooms to the pan and fry for a few minutes, until they begin to soften. Stir in the tomato purée and mustard, then add the crème fraîche. Cook gently, stirring constantly, for 5 minutes.

Stir in the paprika and season to taste with salt and pepper. Garnish with extra paprika and serve immediately.

Beefburgers with Chilli & Basil

Serves 4

650 g/1 lb 7 oz minced beef

1 red pepper, deseeded and
finely chopped

1 garlic clove, finely chopped

2 small red chillies, deseeded
and finely chopped

1 tbsp chopped fresh basil,
plus extra sprigs to garnish

½ tsp ground cumin

salt and pepper

hamburger buns, to serve

Put the minced beef, red pepper, garlic, chillies, chopped basil and
cumin into a bowl and mix until well combined. Season to taste
with salt and pepper. Using your hands, form the mixture into
4 burger shapes.

Cook over a campfire or barbecue for 5–8 minutes on each side,
or until cooked right through. Garnish with sprigs of basil and
serve in hamburger buns.

Beanburgers

Serves 4

420 g/15 oz canned red kidney beans, drained

410 g/14½ oz canned cooked chickpeas, drained

1 egg yolk

¼ tsp smoked paprika

50 g/3½ oz fresh breadcrumbs

3 spring onions, finely chopped

salt and pepper

crusty bread rolls, soured cream, lettuce and sliced tomatoes, to serve

Place the beans and chickpeas in a bowl, stir in the egg yolk, paprika, breadcrumbs and spring onions, and season. Mash together using a potato masher or the back of a fork. The mixture should be mashed just enough so that everything sticks together but retains some of its texture.

Using your hands, form the mixture into 4 burger shapes.

Cook over a campfire or barbecue for 5–8 minutes on each side, or until cooked right through.

Serve in crusty bread rolls with a spoonful of soured cream, plenty of fresh crisp lettuce and some sliced tomatoes.

Honey-glazed Pork Chops

Serves 4

4 lean pork loin chops
4 tbsp clear honey
1 tbsp dry sherry
4 tbsp orange juice
2 tbsp olive oil
2.5-cm/1-inch piece fresh
ginger, grated
sunflower oil
salt and pepper

Season the pork chops with salt and pepper to taste. Reserve while you make the glaze.

To make the glaze, place the honey, sherry, orange juice, half the olive oil and the ginger in a small saucepan. Gently heat over a campfire, stove or barbecue, stirring constantly, until well blended.

Heat the remaining olive oil and the sunflower oil in a large pan and cook the pork chops for 5 minutes on each side.

Brush the chops with the glaze and cook for a further 2–4 minutes on each side, basting frequently with the glaze.

Transfer the pork chops to serving plates and serve hot.

Spicy Tomato Chicken Kebabs

Serves 4

500 g/1 lb 2 oz skinless, boneless chicken breasts

3 tbsp tomato purée

2 tbsp clear honey

2 tbsp Worcestershire sauce

1 tbsp chopped fresh rosemary

250 g/9 oz cherry tomatoes

If using wooden kebab skewers, soak 1 per person in cold water for 30 minutes first to prevent burning.

Using a sharp knife, cut the chicken into small chunks and place in a bowl. Mix together the tomato purée, honey, Worcestershire sauce and rosemary in a separate bowl, then add to the chicken, stirring to coat evenly.

Thread the chicken pieces and cherry tomatoes alternately onto the pre-soaked wooden skewers or metal skewers.

Spoon over any remaining glaze and cook the kebabs over a campfire or barbecue, turning occasionally, until the chicken is cooked through. Serve.

Yakitori Vegetable Kebabs

Serves 4

1 large courgette, sliced

4 spring onions, sliced diagonally

1 orange pepper, deseeded and cubed

100 g/3½ oz button mushrooms, wiped clean

8 cherry tomatoes

Yakitori Sauce

1 tbsp soy sauce

1 tbsp clear honey

1 tbsp rice vinegar

If using wooden kebab skewers, soak 1 per person in cold water for 30 minutes first to prevent burning.

Divide all the vegetables between the pre-soaked wooden skewers or metal skewers, alternating the pieces to make 4 kebabs.

Mix together the yakitori sauce ingredients and drizzle over the kebabs. Cook the kebabs over a campfire or barbecue for about 10–12 minutes until the vegetables are just tender but not soft.

Salmon & Artichoke Packages

Serves 4

4 salmon steaks, about 175 g/
6 oz each

½ lemon, sliced

1 onion, sliced into rings

4 fresh dill sprigs

4 canned artichoke hearts,
drained

4 tbsp olive oil

4 tbsp chopped fresh flat-leaf
parsley

salt and pepper

Cut out 4 squares of double-thickness aluminium foil, each large enough to enclose a fish steak. Place the salmon on the foil and top with the lemon slices, onion rings and dill sprigs. Place an artichoke heart on each salmon steak.

Fold up the sides of the foil. Sprinkle 1 tablespoon of olive oil and 1 tablespoon of parsley into each parcel and season with a little salt and pepper. Fold over the edges of the foil securely.

Cook the fish parcels over a campfire or barbecue for 15 minutes, turning once. Transfer the fish parcels to plates and unwrap. Serve immediately.

Sunshine Risotto

Serves 6

about 12 sun-dried tomatoes

2 tbsp olive oil

1 large onion, finely chopped

4–6 garlic cloves, finely chopped

400 g/14 oz risotto rice

1.5 litres/2¾ pints simmering chicken or vegetable stock

2 tbsp chopped fresh flat-leaf parsley

115 g/4 oz freshly grated Parmesan cheese

salt and pepper

Place the sun-dried tomatoes in a heatproof bowl and pour over enough boiling water to cover. Set aside to soak for 30 minutes or until soft and supple. Drain and pat dry with kitchen paper, then thinly shred and set aside.

Gently heat the oil in a deep saucepan over a campfire, stove or barbecue. Add the onion and cook, stirring occasionally, for 2 minutes or until starting to soften. Add the garlic and cook for a further 15 seconds. Place over a low heat, add the rice and mix to coat in oil. Cook, stirring constantly, for 2–3 minutes or until the grains are translucent.

Gradually add the hot stock, a ladleful at a time. Stir constantly and add more liquid as the rice absorbs each addition. Place over a high heat so that the liquid bubbles. After about 15 minutes, stir in the sun-dried tomatoes and season. Continue adding the stock, stirring constantly, until the risotto has been cooking for 20 minutes or until all the liquid is absorbed and the rice is creamy.

Remove the pan from the heat and stir in the chopped parsley and half the Parmesan cheese. Spoon onto plates and sprinkle the remaining Parmesan cheese on top. Serve.

Chicken Risotto with Saffron

Serves 4

125 g/4½ oz butter

900 g/2 lb skinless, boneless chicken breasts, thinly sliced

1 large onion, chopped

500 g/1 lb 2 oz risotto rice

150 ml/5 fl oz white wine

1 tsp crumbled saffron threads

1.3 litres/2¼ pints simmering chicken stock

55 g/2 oz freshly grated Parmesan cheese

salt and pepper

Heat half of the butter in a deep saucepan over a campfire, stove or barbecue. Add the chicken and onion and cook, stirring frequently, for 8 minutes, or until golden brown.

Add the rice and mix to coat in the butter. Cook, stirring constantly for 2–3 minutes, or until the grains are translucent. Add the wine and cook, stirring constantly, for 1 minute until reduced.

Mix the saffron with 4 tablespoons of the hot stock. Add the liquid to the rice and cook, stirring constantly, until it is absorbed.

Gradually add the remaining hot stock, a ladle at a time. Stir constantly and add more liquid as the rice absorbs each addition. Cook for 20 minutes, or until all the liquid is absorbed and the rice is creamy. Season to taste.

Remove the risotto from the heat and add the remaining butter. Mix well, then stir in the Parmesan until it melts. Spoon the risotto into bowls and serve.

Easy Pizza Calzone

Serves 4

4 flour or corn tortillas

8 tbsp pizza base sauce
(or tomato purée)

200 g/7 oz cooked chicken, finely
shredded

200 g/7 oz mozzarella cheese,
drained and torn into small
pieces

handful basil leaves, torn

salt and pepper

Evenly spread 1 side of each tortilla with 2 tbsp pizza base sauce. Top
with the chicken, mozzarella and basil leaves and season.

Heat a non-stick frying pan over a campfire, stove or barbecue.
Cook 1 calzone at a time in the pan, by first cooking the tortilla for
2 minutes. Then fold in half, press down the edges well to seal and
cook for a further 1 minute on each side. The centre should be piping
hot and the mozzarella starting to melt.

Repeat with the remaining 3 tortillas and serve.

Something On The Side

Garlic Bread

Serves 6

150 g/5½ oz butter, softened

3 cloves garlic, crushed

2 tbsp chopped parsley

pepper

1 large or 2 small sticks
of French bread

Mix together the butter, garlic and parsley in a bowl until well combined. Season with pepper to taste and mix well.

Make several lengthways cuts in the bread but be careful not to cut all the way through.

Spread the flavoured butter over one side of each cut and place the loaf on a large sheet of aluminium foil.

Wrap up the bread in the aluminium foil and cook over a campfire or barbecue for 10–15 minutes, until the butter melts and the bread is piping hot. A classic side dish, which tastes even better cooked in the great outdoors.

Jacket Potatoes

Serves 4

4 large floury potatoes, scrubbed

1 tbsp olive oil

salt

Smoked Mackerel and Soured Cream filling

4 smoked peppered mackerel fillets, skinned

butter

8 tbsp soured cream

pepper

Herby Sausage and Onion filling

1 tbsp olive oil

I red onion, finely chopped

8 pork sausages

handful flat-leaf parsley, finely chopped

tomato relish or salsa, to serve

pepper

Use some clean kitchen paper to rub the potatoes with a little olive oil and sprinkle with salt to coat lightly.

Tightly wrap the potatoes in aluminium foil and cook over a campfire or barbecue (towards the edge, away from the hottest part), for about 1 hour. The cooking time will depend on the size of potato and the strength of the heat from the fire or barbecue. The potato is ready when it yields to the tip of a sharp knife.

To make the smoked mackerel and soured cream filling, simply flake the smoked mackerel, mash with a little butter and serve on the cooked, opened potato. Drizzle over the soured cream and top with pepper.

To make the herby sausage and onion filling, heat the oil in a non-stick frying pan over the campfire, stove or barbecue and sauté the onion for 5–10 minutes. Squeeze the sausage meat out of its casing and add to the pan. Continue to cook until it is browned and thoroughly cooked, breaking it up with a fork as you go. Stir in the parsley. Serve the sausage meat over the cooked potato with some tomato relish or salsa. Season to taste and enjoy.

Meatballs on Sticks

Serves 8

4 pork and herb sausages

115 g/4 oz fresh beef mince

85 g/3 oz fresh white breadcrumbs

1 onion, finely chopped

2 tbsp chopped mixed fresh herbs, such as parsley, thyme and sage

1 egg

sunflower oil, for brushing

salt and pepper

Soak the cocktail sticks in cold water for 30 minutes first to prevent burning.

Remove the sausage meat from the skins, place in a large bowl and break up with a fork. Add the beef mince, breadcrumbs, onion, herbs and egg. Season to taste with salt and pepper and stir well with a wooden spoon until thoroughly mixed.

Form the mixture into small balls, about the size of a golf ball, between the palms of your hands. Spear each one with a cocktail stick and brush with oil.

Cook over a campfire or barbecue, turning frequently and brushing with more oil as necessary, for 10 minutes or until cooked through. Transfer to a plate and serve.

Campfire Chips

Serves 4

12 tbsp olive oil

2 medium sweet potatoes, peeled and cut into thin chips

2 tsp steak seasoning (or use Cajun spice)

salt

garlic mayonnaise, to serve

Heat the oil in a non-stick frying pan over a campfire, stove or barbecue.

Add the chips, scatter over the seasoning and toss well. Gently fry for about 10–12 minutes, turning regularly until the chips are just tender. Serve scattered with salt and some garlic mayonnaise to dip. Absolute heaven!

Campfire Nachos

Serves 4

100 g/4 oz salted tortilla chips

150 g/5 oz cooked chicken, shredded

85 g/3 oz Cheddar cheese, grated

pepper

6 tbsp tomato salsa, to serve

6 tbsp soured cream, to serve

Place a large piece of double-thickness aluminium foil in the base of a non-stick frying pan and place the pan over a campfire, stove or barbecue.

Place the tortilla chips in a single layer on the foil. Scatter over the chicken and cheese. Cover the pan either with a lid or with some foil.

Cook the nachos for about 10–15 minutes until the cheese is just molten (check by opening up the foil regularly).

Season with pepper and serve the nachos with the salsa and soured cream liberally spooned over.

Campfire Roasted Balsamic & Honey Onions

Serves 4

4 red onions, peeled and cut into chunky wedges

4 tsp clear honey

4 tbsp balsamic vinegar

1 tsp fresh thyme, finely chopped

salt and pepper

Divide the onion wedges between 4 squares of double-thickness aluminium foil. Bring up the sides of the foil a little.

Drizzle the honey and balsamic vinegar over the onions, add the thyme and season.

Loosely seal the parcels and cook over a campfire or barbecue for 15–20 minutes until the onions are tender.

Saucy Borlotti Beans

Serves 4–6

600 g/1 lb 5 oz fresh borlotti beans

4 large leaves fresh sage, torn

1 tbsp olive oil

1 large onion, thinly sliced

300 ml/10 fl oz fresh tomato sauce

salt and pepper

Shell the beans. Bring a large saucepan of water to the boil over a campfire, stove or barbecue and add the beans and torn sage leaves. Bring back to the boil, then place over a low heat and simmer for about 12 minutes or until the beans are tender. Drain and set aside.

Gently heat the oil in a large non-stick frying pan. Add the onion and cook, stirring occasionally, for about 5 minutes until softened and translucent, but not browned. Stir the fresh tomato sauce into the pan with the cooked borlotti beans and the torn sage leaves.

Bring to the boil, stirring. Place over a low heat, partially cover and simmer for about 10 minutes, or until the sauce has reduced slightly.

Adjust the seasoning, transfer to a bowl and serve hot.

Peas with Baby Onions

Serves 4

15 g/½ oz unsalted butter
175 g/6 oz whole baby onions
900 g/2 lb fresh peas, shelled
125 ml/4 fl oz water
2 tbsp plain flour
150 ml/5 fl oz double cream
1 tbsp chopped fresh parsley
1 tbsp lemon juice
salt and pepper

Melt the butter in a large, heavy-based saucepan over a campfire, stove or barbecue. Add the baby onions and cook, stirring occasionally, for 5 minutes. Add the peas and cook, stirring constantly, for a further 3 minutes, then add the measured water and bring to the boil. Place over a low heat, partially cover and simmer for 10 minutes.

Beat the flour into the cream. Remove the pan from the heat and stir in the cream mixture and parsley and season to taste.

Return the pan to the heat and cook, stirring gently but constantly, for about 3 minutes, until thickened.

Stir the lemon juice into the sauce and serve the peas immediately.

Parsnip & Potato Rösti

Serves 6

2 large potatoes
2 parsnips
olive oil, for frying
salt and pepper

Peel and grate the potatoes and parsnips onto a clean tea towel. Squeeze out any excess liquid, then spread out onto another clean tea towel or kitchen paper and leave to stand for 10 minutes.

Put the potatoes and parsnips in a bowl, mix together and season to taste with salt and pepper. Gently heat the oil in a non-stick frying pan over a campfire, stove or barbecue. Add a spoonful of the potato mixture, flatten with the back of a spoon to form a rösti and cook for 3–5 minutes until brown and crisp. Carefully turn over and cook for a further 2–3 minutes. Remove and drain on kitchen paper. Wrap the rösti in aluminium foil to keep warm while you cook the remaining parsnip and potato mixture.

Herby Potato Salad

Serves 4–6

500 g/1 lb 2 oz new potatoes

16 vine-ripened cherry
tomatoes, halved

70 g/2½ oz black olives, stoned
and coarsely chopped

4 spring onions, finely sliced

2 tbsp chopped fresh mint

2 tbsp chopped fresh parsley

2 tbsp chopped fresh coriander

juice of 1 lemon

3 tbsp extra virgin olive oil

salt and pepper

Cook the potatoes in a saucepan of lightly salted boiling water over a campfire, stove or barbecue, for 15 minutes or until tender. Drain, then leave to cool slightly. Cut into halves or quarters, depending on the size of the potato. Then combine with the tomatoes, olives, spring onions and herbs in a bowl.

Mix together the lemon juice and oil in a bowl and pour over the potato salad. Season to taste before serving.

Crispy Bacon & Spinach Salad

Serves 4

4 tbsp olive oil

4 rashers of streaky bacon, diced

1 thick slice of white bread, crusts removed, cut into cubes

450 g/1 lb fresh spinach, torn or shredded

Heat 2 tablespoons of the olive oil in a large non-stick frying pan over a campfire, stove or barbecue. Add the diced bacon to the pan and cook for 3–4 minutes, or until crisp. Remove with a slotted spoon, draining carefully, and set aside.

Toss the cubes of bread in the fat remaining in the pan over the heat for about 4 minutes, or until crisp and golden. Remove the croûtons with a slotted spoon, draining carefully, and set them aside.

Add the remaining oil to the frying pan and heat. Toss the spinach in the oil over a high heat for about 3 minutes, or until it has just wilted. Turn into a serving bowl and sprinkle with the bacon and croûtons. Serve immediately.

Corn On The Cob with Blue Cheese Dressing

Serves 6

140 g/5 oz Danish Blue cheese

140 g/5 oz curd cheese

125 ml/4 fl oz natural Greek yogurt

salt and pepper

6 corn cobs in their husks

Crumble the Danish Blue cheese, then place in a bowl. Beat with a wooden spoon until creamy. Beat in the curd cheese until thoroughly blended. Gradually beat in the yogurt and season to taste with salt and pepper. Cover with clingfilm and leave to chill somewhere cool until required.

Fold back the husks on each corn cob and remove the silks. Smooth the husks back into place. Cut out 6 rectangles of double-thickness aluminium foil, each large enough to enclose a corn cob. Wrap the corn cobs in the foil.

Cook the corn cobs over a campfire or barbecue for 15–20 minutes, turning frequently. Unwrap the corn cobs and discard the foil. Peel back the husk on one side of each and trim off with a sharp knife. Serve with the blue cheese dressing.

Garlic Mash

Serves 4

900 g/2 lb floury potatoes, cut into chunks
8 garlic cloves, crushed
150 ml/5 fl oz milk
85 g/3 oz butter
salt and pepper

Place the potatoes in a large saucepan with enough water to cover and a pinch of salt. Bring to the boil over a campfire, stove or barbecue and cook for 10 minutes. Add the garlic and cook for a further 10–15 minutes, or until the potatoes are tender.

Drain the potatoes and garlic, reserving 3 tablespoons of the cooking liquid. Return the reserved cooking liquid to the saucepan, then add the milk and bring to simmering point. Add the butter, return the potatoes and garlic to the saucepan and remove from the heat. Mash thoroughly with a potato masher.

Season the potato mixture and beat thoroughly with a wooden spoon until light and fluffy. Serve immediately and enjoy the ultimate comfort food.

Baked Camembert

Serves 4

1 whole Camembert
(about 200 g/7 oz)
2 cloves garlic, thinly sliced
2 sprigs rosemary, cut into small
pieces
4 tbsp white wine (optional)
salt and pepper
crusty French bread, to serve

Remove the Camembert from its wrapper and place on a piece of double-thickness aluminium foil.

Make about 8–10 small incisions in the surface of the cheese using the tip of a small sharp knife.

Push the garlic slices and rosemary sprigs into the incisions and then drizzle over the wine (if using.) Add a little seasoning.

Loosely seal the foil and then cook directly on the edge of a campfire or barbecue for about 10–15 minutes, depending on the heat levels, until the cheese has become soft and molten in the centre.

Serve with crusty French bread. A real treat for fans of all things cheesy and gooey.

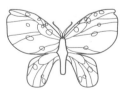

All Things Sweet

Real Hot Chocolate

Serves 1–2

40 g/1½ oz plain chocolate,
broken into pieces
300 ml/10 fl oz milk
chocolate curls, to decorate

Place the chocolate in a large, heatproof jug. Place the milk in a
heavy-based saucepan and bring to the boil over a campfire, stove
or barbecue. Pour about one quarter of the milk onto the chocolate
and leave until the chocolate has softened.

Beat the milk and chocolate mixture until smooth. Return the
remaining milk to the heat and return to the boil, then pour onto
the chocolate, whisking constantly.

Pour into mugs and decorate with chocolate curls. Serve
immediately.

Quick Tiramisu

Serves 4

225 g/8 oz mascarpone or full-fat soft cheese

1 egg, separated

2 tbsp natural yogurt

2 tbsp caster sugar

2 tbsp dark rum

2 tbsp strong black coffee

8 sponge finger biscuits

Put the mascarpone cheese in a large bowl, add the egg yolk and yogurt and beat until smooth.

Whisk the egg white until stiff but not dry, then whisk in the sugar and fold into the mascarpone mixture.

Spoon half of the mixture into 4 glasses.

Mix together the rum and coffee in a shallow dish. Dip the sponge fingers into the rum mixture, break them in half, or into smaller pieces if necessary, and divide between the glasses.

Stir any remaining coffee mixture into the remaining cheese and spoon over the top.

Serve immediately.

Fruit Skewers

Serves 4

a selection of fruit, such as apricots, peaches, strawberries, mangoes, pineapple, bananas, prepared and cut into chunks

maple syrup

50 g/1¾ oz plain chocolate, broken into chunks

If using wooden kebab skewers, soak 1 per person in cold water for 30 minutes first to prevent burning.

Thread alternate pieces of fruit onto the pre-soaked wooden skewers or metal skewers. Brush the fruit with a little maple syrup.

Put the chocolate in a heatproof bowl, set the bowl over a saucepan of barely simmering water and heat over a campfire, stove or barbecue, until the chocolate has melted.

Meanwhile, cook the skewers over the campfire or barbecue for 3 minutes, or until caramelized. Serve drizzled with a little of the melted chocolate.

Orange & Caramel Bananas

Serves 4

115 g/4 oz granulated or caster
sugar

1 tsp vanilla extract

finely grated zest and juice
of 1 orange

4 bananas, peeled and thickly
sliced

2 tbsp butter

Put the sugar, vanilla extract and orange juice in
a non-stick frying pan and gently heat over a
campfire, stove or barbecue, until a caramel
consistency is formed.

Add the banana slices and cook, shaking the pan, for
1–2 minutes until they are coated with the caramel.

Add the butter to the pan and cook for a further
3 minutes, shaking the pan to coat the bananas.

Tip the bananas onto a serving plate and sprinkle
with the orange zest. Serve.

Chocolate Rum Bananas

Serves 4

1 tbsp butter
225 g/8 oz plain or milk
chocolate
4 large bananas
2 tbsp rum
mascarpone cheese, to serve

Take four large squares of double-thickness aluminium foil and brush them with butter.

Cut the chocolate into very small pieces. Carefully make a slit, lengthways, in the peel of each banana, and open just wide enough to insert the chocolate. Place the chocolate pieces inside the bananas, along their lengths, then close them up.

Wrap each stuffed banana in a square of foil and cook over a campfire or barbecue for 5–10 minutes, or until the chocolate has melted inside the bananas. Remove from the heat, place the bananas on plates and pour some rum into each banana.

Serve with mascarpone cheese for a messy but truly indulgent treat.

Chocolate Fondue

Serves 6

18 marshmallows

Fondue
250 g/9 oz plain chocolate,
broken into pieces
150 ml/5 fl oz double cream
2 tbsp brandy

To make the fondue, place the chocolate and cream in a heavy-based saucepan and gently heat over a campfire, stove or barbecue, stirring constantly until the chocolate has melted. Stir in the brandy until thoroughly blended and the chocolate mixture is smooth.

Thread the marshmallows onto wooden or metal skewers and dip into the chocolate fondue.

Crunchy Ginger Apples

Serves 4

2 tbsp lemon juice
2 tbsp butter, melted
2 tbsp demerara sugar
4 crisp, tart apples
4 tbsp diced stem ginger

Place the lemon juice, butter and demerara sugar in three separate small dishes. Dip the cut side of the apples first in the lemon juice, then in the melted butter and, finally, in the sugar.

Cook the apples, cut side down, over a campfire or barbecue for 5 minutes or until the sugar caramelizes and the apple surfaces are dark. Turn and cook for an additional 5 minutes to blacken the skin. The cooked apples should still retain their crunch.

Arrange the apple halves on plates, cut side up, and spoon diced ginger over each half. Serve.

Rice Pudding

Serves 4–6

1 large orange
1 lemon
1 litre/1¾ pints milk
250 g/9 oz short-grain rice
100 g/3½ oz caster sugar
1 vanilla pod, split
pinch of salt
125 ml/4 fl oz double cream
brown sugar, to serve (optional)

Finely grate the rinds from the orange and lemon and set aside. Rinse a heavy-based saucepan with cold water and do not dry it.

Put the milk and rice in the pan and bring to the boil over a campfire, stove or barbecue. Place over a low heat and stir in the caster sugar, vanilla pod, orange and lemon rinds and salt, and simmer, stirring frequently, until the pudding is thick and creamy and the rice grains are tender: this can take up to 30 minutes, depending on how wide the pan is.

Remove the vanilla pod and stir in the cream. Serve at once, sprinkled with brown sugar, if using, or cool completely. The pudding will thicken as it cools, so stir in a little extra milk if necessary before serving.

Chocolate & Marshmallow S'Mores

Serves 4

8 marshmallows

8 digestive biscuits

8 small squares milk chocolate

If using wooden kebab skewers, soak 1 per person in cold water for 30 minutes first to prevent burning.

Thread the marshmallows, 2 at a time, onto the pre-soaked wooden skewers or metal skewers and toast over a campfire or barbecue until they soften.

Place the soft marshmallows onto one biscuit, top with the chocolate squares and sandwich together with the other biscuit. Repeat with the remaining biscuits and marshmallows.

Banana & Dark Chocolate S'Mores

Serves 4

8 marshmallows
8 chocolate cookies
1 banana, thinly sliced
4 squares dark chocolate

If using wooden kebab skewers, soak 1 per person in cold water for 30 minutes first to prevent burning.

Thread the marshmallows, 2 at a time, onto the pre-soaked wooden skewers or metal skewers and toast over a campfire or barbecue until they soften.

Place the soft marshmallows onto 1 cookie, top with a few slices of banana and a square of chocolate, and sandwich together with the other cookie. Repeat with the remaining biscuits and marshmallows. Messy and marvellous!

Chocolate Marshmallow Fudge

Makes about 50 pieces

115 g/4 oz plain chocolate,
broken into pieces

200 g/7 oz white mini
marshmallows

70 g/2½ oz butter, plus extra for
greasing

2 tsp water

115 g/4 oz blanched almonds,
roughly chopped

Put the chocolate in a heatproof bowl, set the bowl over a saucepan of barely simmering water and heat over a campfire, stove or barbecue, until the chocolate has melted. Put the marshmallows, butter and water in a large, heavy-based saucepan and gently heat, stirring frequently, until melted.

Remove the saucepan from the heat and pour the chocolate into the marshmallow mixture. Add the almonds and stir until well mixed.

Pour the mixture into a disposable foil or mess tin container and leave to cool for 1–2 hours until set. Perfect for an energy boost after a long walk.

Raisin Biscuit Cake

Makes about 20 pieces

100 g/3½ oz butter

25 g/1 oz cocoa powder

200 g/7 oz digestive biscuits, crushed

85 g/3 oz raisins or dried cranberries

1 egg, beaten

125 g/4 oz milk chocolate, broken into squares

Melt the butter in a medium-sized saucepan over a campfire, stove or barbecue and stir in the cocoa powder.

Remove from the heat and add the biscuits and dried fruit. Stir well. Allow to cool for 5 minutes.

Add the egg and mix again until thoroughly mixed.

Tip the mixture into a disposable foil or mess tin container. Press down well using the back of a spoon.

Put the chocolate in a heatproof bowl, set the bowl over a saucepan of barely simmering water and heat until the chocolate has melted. Spread evenly over the top of the cake and leave in a cool place to set.

Cut into squares and keep in an airtight container.

Brazil Nut Brittle

Makes about 20 pieces

sunflower oil, for brushing

350 g/12 oz plain chocolate, broken into pieces

100 g/3½ oz shelled Brazil nuts, chopped

175 g/6 oz white chocolate, roughly chopped

175 g/6 oz fudge, roughly chopped

Brush the bottom and sides of a disposable foil container or mess tin with oil.

Melt half the chocolate pieces in a medium-sized saucepan over a campfire, stove or barbecue, and spread in the prepared pan.

Sprinkle with the chopped Brazil nuts, white chocolate and fudge. Melt the remaining chocolate pieces and pour over the top.

Leave in a cool place to set, then break up into jagged pieces using the tip of a strong knife.

Popcorn

Serves 4

1–2 tbsp vegetable oil
75 g popping corn
1 tbsp butter
3 tbsp maple syrup
1 tbsp sesame seeds

Heat the oil in a non-stick saucepan over a campfire, stove or barbecue.

Carefully add the popping corn to the pan in an even layer and cover with a lid.

Cook the popping corn over a gentle heat, shaking the pan occasionally, until the corn kernels pop.

Pour the popcorn into a large mixing bowl, discarding any kernels that may not have popped.

Melt the butter in a small saucepan, then pour in the maple syrup. Bring to the boil, then remove from the heat and cool. Pour the maple syrup sauce over the popcorn, add the sesame seeds and serve.

And finally...

A night under the stars will leave you feeling energized, refreshed and at one with the wonders of nature. In order for others to enjoy the unsurpassable pleasures of camping and to make planning for your next trip that little bit easier, try following these simple suggestions.

Leave your environment exactly as you found it. Collect any rubbish and take it home with you (or dispose of it at your campsite if it has facilities) - always remember to separate out any rubbish that can be recycled.

Collect any dog mess - don't make it someone else's problem.

If your campsite permits campfires, make sure the fire is fully extinguished before you leave it - and on a practical note, make sure you don't light it too near your tent.

Most campsites have a 'no noise after...' rule - much as you may want to continue your campfire chats late into the night, others really don't want to listen, so save the rest of the gossip for over a bacon sandwich in the morning.

If possible, wait for your tent to dry fully before taking it down - if you can't avoid packing up in the rain, make sure the tent is left out to dry as soon as possible when you return home.

Wipe down the base of the tent with a damp cloth when you get back home, and hang to dry over a clothes line. A wet camping trip will result in a very mucky tent - don't wait until your next trip to sort it out.

Store all camping equipment together and in an easily accessible location - so when the sun starts to shine you're ready to go.

Wash any sleeping bags, wipe down airbeds or roll mats and give your camping pots and pans a good scrub as soon as you're back home - all spick and span for your next trip.

Index